RAILS
ACROSS THE NOYO
A RIDER'S GUIDE TO THE SKUNK TRAIN

RAILS
ACROSS THE NOYO
A RIDER'S GUIDE TO THE SKUNK TRAIN

Katy M. Tahja

Tahjanjoki Press
Comptche, California

For information, or to order additional copies, please contact:

Tahjanjoki Press
Post Office Box 194
Comptche, CA 95427
707-937-5854

Cover and interior design: Elizabeth Petersen,
  Mendocino Graphics
Copyediting: Joe Shaw, Cypress House
Illustrations courtesy of Skunk Train Photo Archives,
  California State Library, *Noyo Chief* (now out-of-print),
  Robert Lee, Kelley House Museum, Chuck Hathaway

ISBN 978-0-933391-28-5
Tahjanjoki Press is an imprint of Pacific Transcriptions

FIRST EDITION

2 4 6 8 9 7 5 3 1

Printed in the United States of America, on recycled content paper stock.

DEDICATION

To anyone who ever rode the Skunk Train and thought, "I wish I knew more about…," may you find the answers to your questions here.

To my husband, David Tahja, whose idea of a perfect day is an abandoned railroad grade in the middle of a wilderness—and time to explore it.

TABLE OF CONTENTS

INTRODUCTION

As the conductor called, "All Aboard" and the passengers began climbing onto the Super Skunk Train for their ride through the redwoods, a little boy pulled on his father's hand and asked, "Why do they call it a skunk, Papa? Skunks are fuzzy little animals in the woods. I don't see any skunks here. Why name it a skunk, Papa? I want to know!"

That little fellow isn't alone in his curiosity. Visitors often ask about the origin of the rail line's nickname. Tradition has it that the Skunk name has to do with its odor.

Rail travelers eighty years ago knew what locomotives smelled like: a little oil, a little steam, a lot of hot metal. It was a familiar aroma while boarding a train. But in 1925 something changed here on the North Coast.

While people were adopting cars and highways as the new way to travel, railroads were losing riders. Looking for a new and economical way to move fewer passengers over rail lines, the managers found something different.

This new vehicle looked like a trolley car on iron wheels. It could carry more than twenty passengers with just one operator and was powered by its own gas engine. But when it began running, folks noticed that it didn't smell like a traditional big locomotive. The potbelly stove in the railcar burned crude oil for heat, and it smelled. In truth, people thought that the combined exhaust from the fancy new engine and the smoke from heater's stovepipe smelled like an irritated skunk spraying. That new motorcar stank like a skunk. The nickname stuck.

But a new rail vehicle sometimes becomes so popular with visitors over the years that it outlives all expectations. Forty years later, so many tourists wanted to ride through the redwoods that the Skunk motor car often departed full, leaving unhappy visitors on the station platform unable to get a ride.

The rail line evolved again, and in the 1960s the puffing locomotives and passenger coach cars returned and the train was nicknamed the Super Skunk. Now everyone could catch a ride along the Noyo River and no one got left behind at the depot.

So Papa scooped up the little boy in his arms and said, "Come on, Sonny. Let's board the Super Skunk and go see those big trees." And they did.

NORTH COAST HISTORY

In 1852 a ship named the *Frolic*, laden with trade goods from China, wrecked on the Mendocino Coast near Caspar. The local native people, the Pomo, promptly scavenged the wreck and wrapped themselves in silk shawls, made beads from broken china, and fashioned arrowheads from bottle glass. The Pomo lived in a world rich in plant and animal resources. Occupying inland valleys laden with oaks and acorns, their main food source, they visited the coast to collect seaweed for salt and to gather abalone and seashells. Their lifestyle was about to undergo astonishing changes.

Salvagers from San Francisco came looking for the wreck and found not Chinese treasures but what they called "green gold." Marching down nearly to the surf line were forests of timber just waiting to be logged. The salvagers went back and spread the word.

With the Gold Rush on, there was a tremendous need for building materials in San Francisco. When told about the forest resource, businessmen saw dollar signs on every tree trunk. Sawmills were taken apart in New England, put on ships that sailed around South America, and sent to northern California to be reassembled.

The Northern Pomo had heard about the troubles the arrival of white Americans had brought to tribes farther south and harassed early timber operations in Mendocino, Albion, and along the Noyo River. In 1857 H. G. Gibson was sent to estab-

1

lish an army post a mile north of the Noyo River. He named it after a West Point classmate, Captain Braxton Bragg. Local whites told Gibson they were suffering from "depredations" as Indians "had stolen all they could lay their hands on."

To control the problem, the Mendocino Reservation was established and thousands of Pomo and Yuki natives from as far away as Eureka and Chico were settled on 25,000 acres between the Ten Mile and Noyo rivers. Unfortunately, money provided for food, clothing, and shelter went into the pockets of settlers employed to guard the natives. By 1860, $83,000 had been invested in livestock, improvements, and agricultural implements, but 3,000 natives were not interested in imitating the white man and slipped away.

The Civil War was beginning and troops were needed elsewhere. In 1867 the reservation and post were abandoned and

Before trains began hauling logs out of the woods, oxen did the job. A team waits beside a tree being bucked into logs of movable length. (California State Library)

the land was sold to former reservation employees for $1 an acre.

The first lumber mill was built on the Noyo River in the 1850s, and a two-mile railroad, the Noyo and Pudding Creek, was laid. Change came with the arrival of an individual named C. R. Johnson in 1885. Things took off and Fort Bragg really began to grow.

Young and energetic, C. R. Johnson came from a sawmill-owning family in Wisconsin. He believed that primitive logging operations carried out by manpower and animal power needed to give way to mechanized procedures. Johnson felt that lumber production done right required heavy investments of money and operations on a massive scale if it was to be profitable.

In 1885 Johnson organized the Fort Bragg Lumber Company near the site of the abandoned military post, founded the Fort Bragg Railroad, and incorporated the town of Fort Bragg. By 1889 he was the mayor. C. R. was the kind of man who liked to get things done as efficiently as possible and surrounded himself with people who knew how to make it happen. He liked good, dependable workers who knew their jobs. Johnson wanted to create community, and his first responsibility was to keep family men and old-timers employed. During the economic depression in the woods between 1924 and 1938, wages might be only eighteen cents an hour, but at least there would be some work for these folks.

The first locomotive, the *Sequoia*, couldn't be delivered by ship until a wharf was built in Soldiers Harbor and laid with track. The *Sequoia* arrived in 1886, and the tracks that would one day be the Skunk Train line began creeping into the timberlands to the east. By 1887 the rails reached almost seven miles to Glen Blair, and a second engine arrived with a passenger coach for rail service. With the need for more investors to extend the railroads and bring more logs to the mill, the Union

Fort Bragg Railroad's first engine, Sequoia, *built in 1885. (California State Library)*

Lumber Company was formed in 1891. In 1893, Chinese laborers, who had learned their tunneling skills working on the transcontinental railroad, completed a tunnel fourteen feet wide and 1,184 feet long to reach the Noyo River drainage timberlands.

By 1896, Union Lumber Company was cutting one third of Mendocino County's lumber output. While railroads were built for industrial support, passenger excursions on Sundays were popular with loggers and their families, and all travelers looked forward to the day when a local train would connect with a main-line carrier and a person could take a train from Fort Bragg to San Francisco.

By 1904 the tracks had reached Alpine at milepost 18 where passengers boarded a buckboard stagecoach to cross the mountain divide and continue on the Willits and inland routes. In 1905 the railroad became its own entity when Union Lumber Company created the California Western Railroad and

Construction crews pause during grading work in 1910.
(California State Library)

Navigation Company. Navigation? On a railroad? The California Western connected to steamships providing transportation to the Bay Area for passengers, lumber, freight, and mail. The railroad never operated the ships, but it owned the wharf at Soldiers Harbor and had jurisdiction over loading ships.

The Great San Francisco Earthquake of 1906 wreaked havoc on the mill, the town of Fort Bragg, and the railroad. In the aftermath of the quake, fire threatened the mill and town but a locomotive under steam at the time sped to the scene in town and provided power for pumping water from the mill pond to the firefighters' hoses. Fires had to be put out at the mill too.

All the coastal lumber mills got a boost from that quake, as San Francisco used redwood lumber to rebuild thousands of buildings. C. R. Johnson threw open the doors of the Company Store and the mill yard, inviting survivors to help themselves to needed supplies for which they could pay the company later. The cargo of supplies aboard the first steamer arriving

Workers take a break from laying track on a steep hillside.
(Skunk Train Archive)

Five logs from one redwood tree arriving at the Fort Bragg mill in
1910. (California State Library)

6

from the south was shared with every mercantile in town, not just the Company Store—that's the kind of businessman C. R. was. The year 1906 also saw the conversion of California Western's locomotives from wood burning to using oil for fuel.

Work on the railroad progressed slowly as economic booms and busts alternated. Construction costs were high, the work was tedious, and tracks had to cross and re-cross the Noyo River. Supporting timbers for bridges could not go underneath the roadbed because many logs floated down the rivers in wintertime, so A-frame bridges, which carried stress on beams atop the structures, were used to avoid river debris.

Annual rainfall was often in excess of 50 inches, causing washouts and landslides, derailing locomotives, and closing the rail line for months at a time. But the California Western kept inching down the canyons and, in 1908, reached Irmulco at Milepost 23.9.

California Western Railroad grades were steep, up to 3.3 percent as compared with one percent on most railroads, and curves were often a tight 33 degrees. One stretch of track twisted eight miles to cover a distance of one-and-a-half miles.

Profits from the timber logged and sent by rail to the Union Lumber Company mill in Fort Bragg kept the tracks progressing. By 1910 Burbeck was reached at Milepost 27.8. Now the really hard construction work began.

Although Burbeck was only five miles as the crow flies from the proposed terminus in Willits, construction engineers announced that the mountains were so steep it would take twelve miles of track to reach Willits. By 1911 passenger service extended from Fort Bragg to Soda Springs at Milepost 28.7 where an auto stage took travelers on to Willits. It took five months to build a second tunnel, 795 feet long, near the summit.

7

On December 11, 1911, the brass band tuned up and the celebration began as folks celebrated the line's completion. Fort Bragg residents considered it a great Christmas present and everyone wanted to ride that first train over the hill. C. R. Johnson got to choose the 150 lucky folks. Since Engine 5 had only two passenger coaches for dignitaries, those extra passengers happily rode over the hill seated on benches nailed onto flatcars.

Despite the completion of the line, it would be June 25, 1912 before regularly scheduled passenger service commenced with a two-and-a-half-hour ride. The track needed ballasting with gravel, a rough winter followed, Tunnel No. 2 caught fire, and 400 feet of track had to be replaced. Fort Bragg cheered the arrival of eighty-two barrels of wine from Cloverdale on July 27, 1912.

Every railroad in America drew new settlers into its area and this train was no exception. What better use for cutover timberland than to sell it to settlers and investors as property perfect for development into homes? Union Lumber Company sold cleared land along the tracks for residential, dairy, and orchard use, with telephone lines available.

Northwestern Pacific, the train line from Eureka to Tiburon, was completed in 1914 with a golden spike at Cain Rock in Humboldt County, and in 1915 local lumber mills set aside clear-grain redwood with no imperfections or knots for construction of the Willits station to serve both railroads. The station had Tyrolean lines of architecture, like a mountain lodge, and in 1916 the interior was paneled in beautiful wood. Since neither train line had dining cars, a dining room for passengers was built into the station.

Pullman sleeping-car service between Fort Bragg and Tiburon began May 22, 1921 when night passenger service began. Leaving at 9:00 p.m., the California Western cars were added

*Train crew in front of Engine 5 more than one hundred years ago.
(California State Library)*

A 1917 publicity brochure for the California Western Railroad extols camping, hunting, and fishing in the redwoods. (Skunk Train Archive)

to Northwestern Pacific's night train at Willits and arrived in San Francisco at 9:00 a.m. The cookhouse at Northspur's logging camp made doughnuts and coffee for late-night treats.

To Union Lumber Company, the California Western Railroad was an industrial tool built and expanded to bring loggers into uncut timber and haul the logs they felled back to the mill in Fort Bragg to be made into lumber. The last thing they wanted was to run a passenger service, but the public clamored for it, so the CWR became a passenger railroad too. No ridership numbers were kept until after 1904, and such numbers have always been deceptive, since loggers riding back and forth to logging sites were included in passenger numbers.

In 1923, 38,000 people rode the California Western— double the number of four years before. Change was on the way, the age of the automobile was arriving, and train ridership began decreasing. Throughout the 1920s the volume of passengers declined. California Western Railroad looked to ways of reducing the cost without sacrificing rail service to passengers.

Even if there were just a handful of people on board, a passenger train back then required a locomotive, a coach, and an engineer, fireman, conductor, and brakeman. Motor-vehicle manufacturers offered railroads an interesting alternative mode of transportation to try out.

Mack Motor Cars mounted a gasoline-powered bus vehicle on rail wheels. The rail bus was cheap and easy to operate. A battery-powered self-starter turned the engine over, the gears shifted like a car, and it had quick power for faster stops and starts. A rail bus required less maintenance than a locomotive and coach, and needed only an engineer and a conductor. It cost California Western $12,524 to purchase one in 1925. Designated M-80, it was thirty-eight feet long and featured a baggage compartment and a toilet. Locals thought its gas fumes stank; hence, it was nicknamed the "Skunk."

By November 1929 the Pullman night-train service ended due to poor ridership, but the Skunk car was proving a hit. A second rail bus, M-100, was added in 1936 so repairs to a motorcar could be made without temporarily firing up a steam locomotive for passenger service.

The Great Depression slowed railroad and logging activities on the Mendocino Coast. Timber around Northspur was logged out; timber cutting moved to Shake City and continued until 1933. The mill in Fort Bragg kept operating, though at reduced output. The last of the steam lumber schooners ceased operation in 1939. That same year C. R. Johnson retired after fifty-seven years in the lumber industry. A small collection of steam locomotives

Motorcar M-100 outside the engine house in Fort Bragg. (Skunk Train Archive)

handled nightly freight between Union Lumber Company's mill and the Northwestern Pacific connection in Willits, and took care of local switching at the mill.

Engine 45 under restoration in the shop. (Skunk Train Archive)

C. R. Johnson had been an innovator, developing the best sawmill equipment, reducing waste, and experimenting with reforestation. In 1922 he started tree nurseries and later created tree farms. He supported tractor logging and selective cutting, leaving big trees for conservationists' and tourists' approval and enjoyment.

In 1937 Union Lumber Company experimented with shredded redwood bark as insulation, used waste wood for shingles, fence posts, and firewood, and wood chips for paper stock. Johnson, a philanthropist, gave over 2,000 acres of land along the rail lines to the Boys and Girls Clubs and Boy Scouts for summer camp, facilities that are still used to this day.

Prior to World War II a combination baggage-passenger car was carried on the night freight train to Willits to maintain passenger service, but this ended in October 1937. Motorcar M-200 was purchased in 1941 and was a giant—twice as big as M-80.

In the 1940s the woods' camps with housing ended and loggers were brought to work in the woods by a bus. Diesel locomotives slowly replaced steam locomotives, and by 1952 seven steam locomotives had been scrapped. Soon only one remained as a spare in case a diesel electric locomotive was down, but later it too was gone.

By the 1950s the outside world had gotten word about the availability of a unique train ride through the redwoods on a funny motorcar called the Skunk. National Geographic did a feature on the train in May 1959, and Sunset Magazine did feature articles too. Ridership of 13,000 in 1953 grew to 37,000 in 1959, when a cute little cartoon skunk was added to the motorcars.

While transporting tourists was a moneymaker, the Skunk always took care of those folks who lived along the line. Groceries and newspapers were distributed and medicines delivered. Mail and packages were delivered to eighteen stations. Hikers, fishermen, and campers were picked up and dropped off along the way. At one point 2,500 people had camps, homesteads, and leaseholds along the California Western line. A fourth motorcar, M-300, was added in 1963, and annual ridership grew to 44,000.

Advertisement in an issue of the **Wall Street Journal** *from 1954. (Skunk Train Archive)*

Did you know that the California Western line has been in many movies? In 1948 it was used in *Johnny Belinda*, and in 1974 in *Runaway on the Rogue River*, complete with an elephant in the Noyo River. You can see it in *Racing With the Moon*, filmed in 1984, when movie-studio money helped finance the rebuilding of Engine 45.

Sometimes fame can mean too much of a good thing: tourists were flocking to the coast to ride the Skunk Train, but the motorcars were so packed with riders that disappointed folks were left behind on the depot boarding ramp.

Profits were eluding the California Western because motorcars couldn't carry enough passengers to offset the cost of maintaining the right-of-way, which was plagued by floods and landslides. Sometimes going back to the old ways is the best solution, and bringing back steam locomotives and passenger coaches looked enticing.

So where do you find used steam locomotives in the 1960s? In Oregon. And where do you find used passenger coaches short enough to negotiate California Western's tight curves? In Pennsylvania. What do you call this new train? The Super Skunk. On July 10, 1965 it steamed into service. Super Skunks ran during the summer on excursions, and rail buses ran during the winter. For economy, diesel locomotives pulled many of the Super Skunks in later years.

North Coast weather can severely damage a rail line, and in March 1974 heavy rains and flooding destroyed a bridge, structurally weakened two more, and swept away or buried several miles of track under rocks and mud. It took fifty days to reopen the line. In October of that year something that hadn't happened in six years occurred: trains loaded with logs came rolling into Fort Bragg! Those winter storms had brought

down 450 trees along the tracks, and to prevent logjams occurring under bridges, the logs were gathered using Georgia Pacific loaders and cranes mounted on railcars. This yielded nine trains, each seven log cars long, loaded with

M-300 Motorcar in the shadows at Northspur. (Skunk Train Archive)

14

Engines 64 and 45 in Fort Bragg; new motive power and old. (Skunk Train Archive)

second-growth timber, which produced 98,000 board feet of lumber.

The Skunk line was one of the last railroads in America to deliver mail on a regular basis. It was a rural route deliverer and the U.S. Postal Service sent a movie crew out to document it but this service had ceased by year 2003.

Changes were afoot in the lumber industry too. In 1970, Boise Cascade Corporation acquired Union Lumber Company and the California Western Railroad, then sold them to Georgia Pacific Corporation in 1973. In 1977 Georgia Pacific leased the train to the Mendocino Coast Railway, which sold it in 1987 to Kyle Railways. A group of local Mendocino Coast businessmen bought the Skunk Train in the 1990s, but with the closing of the Georgia Pacific mill in 1998 and the attendant loss of freight revenue, the train line went into bankruptcy in 2002. It looked like the Skunk Train might really be at the end of the line.

In December 2003, Sierra Railroad came to the rescue. An experienced tourist rail operator with the successful Sierra Railroad Dinner Train in the Sierra foothills, they provided the capital improvements needed to reinvigorate the rail line. Ridership is up, marketing has increased, and the Sierra operation allows centralized functions and planning. The Skunk Train is no longer a stand-alone operation but part of a family of well-run entertainment train rides. In June 2005 *Sunset* magazine named the Skunk Train one of the ten best rail journeys in America.

Excursion train over a trestle on the Ten Mile Line in 1949, pulled by Engine 14. (Noyo Chief *Photo*)

TRACKSIDE HISTORY

Below, the first number you see is the distance in miles from the Fort Bragg Station. The number in parentheses is the distance from the Willits station. CWR is the California Western Railroad—the Skunk Train. ULC is the Union Lumber Company.

MP 0 (40) FORT BRAGG... The depot, built in 1924, faces onto Laurel Street, which was the northern boundary of the military post established here in 1857. Alder Street on the south, McPherson Street on the east, and the train and mill yard to the west completed the boundaries. Many of the buildings facing Main Street date from the 1880s and were saloons, restaurants, and general stores.

At the end of the block to the south is the Company Store, built in 1892 by Union Lumber Company to serve loggers, mill employees, and the public. Built of beautifully milled redwood, it had a meat market and a grocery store, and sold hardware, clothing, furniture, candy, stationary, appliances, and floor coverings. The packaging department prepared deliveries for logging camps and families living along the CWR line. Today the building is still full of interesting shops and restaurants.

The Guest House is a Victorian mansion built in 1892 as "The Cottage" for the C. R. Johnson family. In 1912 it became the Guest House for visitors to ULC operations and served that purpose until 1969. Constructed entirely of redwood, it had five bedrooms, extensive kitchen facilities, and rooms for the housekeeper. It features ornate woodwork done by local artisans of the time, as well as twelve-foot ceilings and two fireplaces.

After crossing Main Street the train passes the cemetery, the resting place of many generations of trainmen and loggers. You are about to enter a world without automobiles. The next highway is 37.5 miles ahead.

MP 1 (39) PUDDING CREEK... You've been traveling along Pudding Creek. The pond area was used for log storage in years gone by but is now a wildlife area for waterfowl, turtles, and herons. Ospreys nest in this area. Pilings that used to support trestles remain visible.

MP 3.4 (36.1) GLEN BLAIR JUNCTION... The track here can be several feet under water during winter flooding, as the elevation is only twenty-seven feet above sea level. (It was eighty feet back at the depot). Rails led off here to the Glen Blair Mill where more than ten miles of logging railroad spread through

Diesel excursion moving up the Noyo River. (Skunk Train Archive)

the woods. The Glen Blair Mill functioned from 1886 until 1928, with 250 employees, family houses, and a school. Rails were pulled up in January 1942, and the mill was scrapped in 1947.

TUNNEL NUMBER ONE... Built in 1893, the tunnel is 1,184feet long and cuts through the ridge separating the Pudding Creek and Noyo River watersheds. It was completed by Chinese laborers who had learned their craft working on the transcontinental railroad. Water-pumping intakes for the city of Fort Bragg are just east of the tunnel.

MP 5.8 (34.2) HAY SHED SIDING... There was once a bridge across the river here. Perhaps it ran past a home's barn and hay shed. Now there's a U.S. Geologic Survey gauging station here.

Engine 45 steaming along the line. (Photo by Chuck Hathaway)

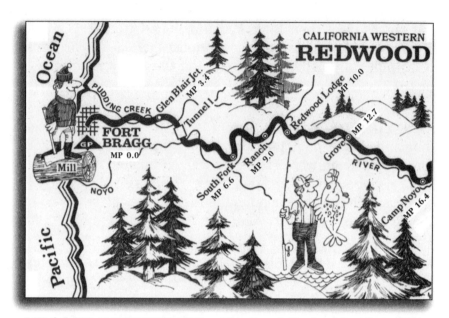

MP 6.6 (33.4) SOUTH FORK... The South Fork of the Noyo River enters the main stream here. In 1887, before it was logged off, the area was a popular destination for Sunday excursion trains from Fort Bragg, A spur ran down to the river where a dragline scooped up gravel to be used for track-bed maintenance.

MP 7.3 (32.7) ROCKPIT... A straightforward name for what was found here. If CWR needed rock for filling holes they got it here.

MP 9.0 (31) COMPANY RANCH... ULC raised beef and mutton here to supply the logging camp cookhouses and the butcher shops in Fort Bragg. ULC built Riverside School for families in the area. Stumps were burned after logging took place to keep them from re-sprouting.

MP 10 (30) REDWOOD LODGE... The Redwood Lodge Resort burned here in 1963, but the pretty little station with squared

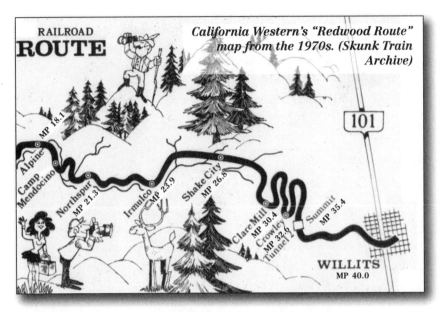

RAILROAD
ROUTE

California Western's "Redwood Route" map from the 1970s. (Skunk Train Archive)

101

MP 18.1
Alpine
Camp
Mendocino
Northspur
MP 21.3
Irmulco
MP 23.9
Shake City
MP 26.8
Clare Mill
MP 30.4
Crowley
MP 32.6
Tunnel 2
Summit
MP 35.4

WILLITS
MP 40.0

redwood timbers remains. Railroad construction crews reached this spot on the Little North Fork of the Noyo River in 1888. ULC's owner chose this area to start a tree nursery in 1922. Replanting baby redwoods failed due to fire, rodents, and dry years, but baby Douglas fir survived when planted. It was discovered that over 90 percent of logged redwoods re-sprout and grow new trees, making redwood the fastest-growing softwood lumber resource. In May 1951 ULC designated 65,331 acres as the C. R. Johnson Tree Farm.

MP 12.7 (27.3) GROVE... Notice the springboard sticking out of the tree? Redwood stumps are high because the tree is heavier toward the butt where water is retained. This made logs sink when they were floated downriver toward the mill. Scars in the bark of the tree indicate that wire rigging was once attached to it. A core sampling by professional foresters showed the tree was more than 1,000 years old. Just east of Grove the train will slow down for a "Kodak Moment" as you pass one of the oldest trees along the line.

21

ELEVATIONS OF THE SKUNK LINE

Distance (miles)	Station	Elevation (feet above sea level)
0.0	Fort Bragg	80
1.0	Pudding Creek	20
3.4	Glen Blair Junction	27
6.6	South Fork	39
9.0	Ranch	64
10.0	Redwood Lodge	78
12.7	Grove	125
15.0	Camp Three	199
16.0	Camp Four	228
16.4	Camp Noyo	229
18.1	Alpine	264
20.0	Camp Seven	292
20.5	Noyo Lodge	308
21.3	Northspur	322
23.9	Irmulco	408
26.8	Shake City	560
27.7	Burbeck	688
28.7	Soda Spring	808
30.4	Clare Mill	1,023
32.6	Crowley	1,375
33.8	Crater	1,513
35.4	Summit	1,740
37.5	Rodgers	1,433
40.0	Willits	1,364

MP 15 (25) CAMP THREE... This was the site of one of the logging and construction camps as the rail line worked its way east. Homes and orchards are occasionally visible. Groceries would be packed at the Company Store in Fort Bragg and dropped off at stations closest to a homeowner's cabin.

MP 16 (24) CAMP FOUR... Another work camp. These camps would last three months to a year until the trees were logged and the railroad crews moved east. This rail line would never have been built if money from the trees logged, cut into lumber, and sold had not been an ongoing source of income for ULC. An old, destroyed cabin is visible in the brush.

A Skunk motorcar stops to pick up mail along the route.
(Skunk Train Archive)

23

MP 16.4 (23.6) CAMP NOYO... Camp Noyo is the name for the Boy Scout Camp over a bridge on the south side of the river. It was formerly called Camp Silverado.

MP 18.1 (21.9) ALPINE... The train has gained 200 feet in elevation in two miles. Can you imagine hundreds of people living and working here? In 1904 it was a busy place with Duffy's Hotel, a tavern, a post office, and a school from 1905 to 1918. Everything burned in 1919. When CWR tracks ended here you could take a stagecoach onward to Sherwood and Willits twenty-three miles away.

MP 19.0 (21.0) CAMP MENDOCINO... Occupying 2,000 acres on both sides of the track here, Camp Mendocino belongs to the Boys and Girls Club of San Francisco. Two thousand kids, ages six to fourteen, enjoy a summer of fun here; since 1931 more than 65,000 children have visited. It used to be called

Boy Scouts leave the train at Camp Noyo for an outdoor adventure. (Skunk Train Archive)

A patriotic Skunk engine at Northspur. (Skunk Train Archive)

Camp Marwedel. Off-season the camp is the western-region training center for Americorps.

MP 20 (20) CAMP SEVEN... Another center for logging activity in 1915, then it was gone.

MP 21.3 (18.7) NORTHSPUR... The halfway point for the ride to Willits has one of the three wyes (Y's) on the track for turning the locomotive around. Most private homes here are up the North Fork of the Noyo River, and this used to be the home of the Noyo River Apple Company. Camp Saint Alberts (also called Albertinium) was here, and it was a quarter mile to the Noyo River Tavern. The cookhouse was part of the section-crew housing maintained here over fifty years ago.

MP 23.9 (16.1) IRMULCO... If you take the first two letters from the words "Irvine & Muir" and add "lco" for lumber company you get Irmulco. Home of the Irvine & Muir Lumber Company in 1908, it supported thirteen miles of logging railroads up the canyons. A school served the area from 1909 to 1927. There was a mill, store, cookhouse, family houses, and bunkhouses. More than 150 people lived here. A road from Highway 20 drops down to Irmulco.

MP 24.5 (15.5) REDWOOD CREEK... The mill at Irmulco cut timber in this area and, in later years, another mill operated here. An oldtimer living in Irmulco would come down the track every morning to build a fire in the schoolhouse to warm it for the loggers' children.

MP 26.4 (13.6) MCMULLEN CREEK... In 1957 the last train to pull nothing but logs for the mill left in January. After that CWR hauled nothing but freight and passengers. From here

Tracks curve around on themselves near Crowley. This view is now hidden by brush and trees. (Skunk Train Archive)

travelers are on the only single mile of straight track on the entire forty miles of line to Willits.

MP 26.8 (13.2) SHAKE CITY... Workers split shakes for roofing here before it was destroyed by fire in the 1950s. The CWR climbs a 2.6 percent grade here headed for the summit eight miles away.

MP 27.8 (12.3) BURBECK... You've climbed one hundred feet since Shake City. From here Willits is five air miles away but twelve track miles. Some of ULC's last logging along the line was done here in 1968.

MP 28.7 (11.3) SODA SPRING... You've climbed 400 feet in the last five miles. The horseshoe curve is coming up with some spectacular views downhill, but timber and brush have grown up and block what was once a twisting, turning track view.

MP 30.4 (9.6) CLARE MILL... There once was a railroad tie mill here; now there's a weathered sign. Old cabins may be visible downhill. The old stagecoach route crosses the tracks. A bridge here was 600 feet long and seventy-three feet high, with twenty-four-degree turns, but it was replaced with earth fill in 1936. Two miles to Crowley and 350 feet to climb.

MP 32.6 (7.4) CROWLEY... Collapsed cabins of track workers can be seen here. At MP 32.83 (7.2) a trestle burned in April 1949, and cribbing with three-foot-wide logs forty feet long held fill so track could be re-laid. Now it's called Rockwall.

MP 33.8 (6.2) CRATER... At this cut you're climbing at a three percent grade headed for Tunnel Number Two and the summit, gaining another 227 feet.

Engine 21 near the summit of the Coast Range in winter snows.
(Skunk Train Archive)

TUNNEL NUMBER TWO... Completed in 1911 it removed the last barrier as CWR headed to Willits and is 812 feet long.

MP 35.4 (4.6) SUMMIT... You're now at 1,740 feet—the top of the Coast Range. In 1970, on the other side of the summit, three diesels, Numbers 51, 52, and 54, lost their air brakes and went racing down the 3.5 percent grade towards Willits until they derailed. No one was hurt.

MP 37.5 (2.5) RODGERS... The CWR crosses Highway 20 here and may stop at the KOA campground for passengers.

MP 38.6 (1.4) SAGE SPUR... Site of another lumber mill, this is halfway between the Highway 20 crossing and the Highway 101 crossing. Black Bart Indian Gaming Casino is just down the road.

MP 40 (0) WILLITS... The depot was built in 1915 of choice clear-grain redwood provided by ULC and other mills. Northwestern Pacific Railroad used to provide passenger and freight service from Eureka to the Bay Area, but landslides in the Eel River canyon to the north have now closed the line. Rail enthusiasts and mass-transit fans hope it will be opened from here south someday.

The Mendocino County Museum is just a few blocks to the east on Commercial Street. It offers more information on rail history and displays steam-powered logging equipment operated by Roots of Motive Power during special events. Within walking distance there are many shops and dining establishments and city parks to picnic in.

Rails vanish into the woods along the Noyo. Note insulators for phone lines on a cross-arm nailed to a tree. (Skunk Train Archive)

NATURE ALONG THE SKUNK LINE

The tallest living things on earth surround you when you ride the Skunk Train through forests of coast redwoods on the "Redwood Route."

Growing over 350 feet tall, these redwoods can survive 500 to 1,000 years or more and grow in a coastal maritime climate. Fossil records show ancestor redwoods were growing when dinosaurs walked the earth. Changing climates now limit redwoods to three places on earth, where three species grow.

China has dawn redwoods, *Metasequoia glyptostroboides*, and central California's Sierra has giant Sequoia, *Sequoiadendron giganteum*. The north coast of California and southern Oregon is home to the coast redwood, *Sequoia sempervirens*.

Coast redwoods love summer fog and winter rains. The tree is rich in tannin that makes the wood, bark, and foliage resistant to insect and fungal damage. With no resin or pitch, they are protected from wildfire and they can survive a long, long time—stumps with 2,200 annual growth rings have been found.

Journals of white European explorers noted that Juan Cabrillo of Portugal first saw the great trees in 1542, and England's Sir Francis Drake observed them in 1579. In 1769, Father Juan Crespi, a Catholic missionary, called them *palo colorado*—red wood. When Russian fur traders built a fort on the Sonoma coast in 1812 they used redwood lumber. Fort Ross still stands.

31

For such a giant tree, coast redwoods have tiny cones, about the size of an olive. Inside the cones are over 100 seeds, each about the size of a tomato seed. An old-growth redwood can produce 100,000 cones a year. Getting a new start on life, seedlings have only a ten percent chance of survival, but Mother Nature helped out with another adaptation.

Coast redwoods can develop root burls—a mass of matter like a wart or canker—capable of producing sprouts, and a ring of smaller trees can grow around the parent tree. If a tree is cut down, the mature root system left behind nurtures sprouts. Root-collar sprouts around a tree's base can survive to maturity and make new trees. Burls can also grow on the trunks of trees, high above the forest floor, and eventually weigh thousands of pounds. Burlwood is beautifully patterned and is popular for making redwood novelties.

Originally, coast redwoods covered two million acres of north coast land. Today 80,000 acres of old-growth forest survive in parks and 7,000 acres are in private lands. Only four percent of the original virgin redwood forests remain. The forests along the Skunk Train line are owned by lumber companies and feature second- and third-growth timber resources. Redwoods growing in the Noyo River watershed grow taller, loggers say, because of the steep sides of the canyon. Redwoods in the Big River and Ten Mile River watersheds are bigger around because they grow on flat, wide river banks.

While coast redwoods surround the Skunk Train tracks, other plants and trees also adorn the landscape. Douglas fir is harvested for lumber, and several varieties of oak love the open meadows. Alder, sycamore, tan oak, buckeye, bay laurel, Pacific dogwood, and big leaf maple grace the forest, together with western hemlock, white fir, and chinquapin oak. Rhododendrons and azaleas bloom in spring, and poison oak foliage turns red in the fall. Wildflowers include wild lilies, lupine, poppies, iris, Indian paintbrush, and a wide variety of ferns. Often searched for but seldom seen is the tiny Calypso orchid.

A variety of wildlife inhabits the coast redwood forest. Most of these creatures stay hidden during the daytime. Marbled murreletes and northern spotted owls roost in the trees, as do red tree voles and northern flying squirrels. Beavers have been reported in the South Fork, and river otters splash about. Pacific giant salamanders, up to twelve inches long, hide under logs, and blacktail deer browse open meadows. Occasionally, elk are seen. Raccoons and skunks move about in the underbrush, as do bobcats. Turkey vultures circle in the sky, and red-tailed hawks swoop down on mice. Bluejays and wild turkeys might be seen anywhere, and ravens watch from the tree branches. Ducks swim on the river's surface, and salmon swim beneath it with other trout to keep them company. Bears and mountain lions are present but very rarely seen.

RACCOON STORY

The Skunk Train always took care of the families living along the tracks and sometimes it was animal families.

More than fifty years ago the night freight train on the California Western stopped at Clare Mill to take on water. While this chore was being done the crew ate their lunches and threw edible remains into the brush.

A raccoon soon realized that food appeared when the train stopped, and learned to wait for the handout. The mama raccoon became so tame she would accept tidbits from the engineer's hand, and when she had babies, called cubs, she brought them to the tracks for free food too.

Through the years, the descendants of that original mama raccoon had lunch with the crew at Clare Mill, but then the freight

no longer needed to stop there and the crew had a lunch stop in Willits. Horrors! Starving raccoons? No, don't worry.

The raccoons, being intelligent little creatures, discovered that the train now switched out loaded log cars and replaced them with empties at Burbeck station, where more friendly train crews with lunch scraps stopped. The mama coons and their cubs just moved west down the hill to Burbeck.

Brazen raccoons would climb right into the locomotive cab. Engineers brought more diced old bread for their "dinner guests." Crews shared the job of providing raccoon treats. This tradition went on for more than eight years.

GEOLOGY ALONG THE SKUNK LINE

What's under all these trees and the river? Mendocino County is part of the continental overthrust zone, where the Pacific tectonic plate has collided with the North American plate, and the San Andreas fault line lies just offshore. The Noyo River watershed comprises 113 square miles of land extending from sea level to 3,207 feet elevation at Sherwood Peak.

Raised marine terraces spread from the Pacific shore to the 650-foot elevation heading east; these are composed of sandstone, shale, and conglomerate. Inland the bedrock is Franciscan formation, a mixture of rock fragments of various ages and origins. It is highly fractured and deformed by folding, faulting, and metamorphism, with graywacke the predominant rock.

This is a highly unstable, weathered rock, and the combination of steep slopes and high rainfall makes mudflows, rockslides, and slumping earth a common wintertime occurrence. Skunk Train track-maintenance workers fight a constant battle to keep the dirt and rock where it belongs—off the tracks.

California Western rail bridge burning at MP 13.27 between Grove and Camp Three October 15, 1951. (Skunk Train Archive)

TRIVIA ONLY A RAILFAN WOULD LOVE

The Skunk Train route had more bridges per mile than perhaps any other railway in America. In 1922 there were 115 bridges; today there are thirty. It takes forty rail miles to cover the twenty-two air miles from Fort Bragg to Willits. There used to be 381 curves in the track. The rail line was built to standard gauge so it could easily connect to transcontinental lines.

California Western owned twenty steam locomotives before converting to diesel electric motors.

Motorcars used twenty-five gallons of gas for an eighty-mile roundtrip; when converted to diesel they used only ten gallons of fuel. Diesel locomotive engines use 150 gallons of fuel for the trip. Engine 45 uses 400 gallons of filtered, recycled motor oil for fuel; it eats up eight gallons a mile and needs 2000 gallons of water.

To appease superstitious passengers and railway employees there has never been an Engine 13.

For thirty-five years there was no regularly scheduled steam passenger service on the California Western line.

In 1904 the combined railroad and stagecoach fare from Fort

Bragg to Willits and down to Ukiah, the county seat, was $8.50. The rail fare from Ukiah to San Francisco was only $4.50. Roundtrip rail fare from Fort Bragg to Willits in 1956 was $3.45.

From 1916 to 1949 the California Western had a twenty-two-mile-long branch railroad up the Ten Mile River. In one month, from June to July 1949, the rails were torn up and the grade was turned into a high-speed truck road.

Storms in 1906 washed out eight bridges; it took three months to reopen the line.

Hollywood needed two engines in the 1984 movie *Racing With the Moon*. They changed the number and moved the headlight on Engine 45 to make it do double duty. Movie crews shot night-time scenes on a ninety-degree day in Willits using filters to darken the daylight. The movie studio also paid thousands of dollars to restore Engine 45 for use in that movie.

W-111B Hydraulic Track Liner measures track for adjustment east of Ranch station in 1970. (Noyo Chief *Photo)*

TrainSinger® Greg Schindel performing at Northspur.

Always a crowd pleaser, singer Greg Schindel, also known as TrainSinger®, has ridden the Skunk since 1988, playing traditional train songs on guitar, harmonica, and whistle. His CDs reflect the history of railroad music.

In years past, Model Engineer Works of Monrovia California provided an HO scale Skunk M-80 railcar for model railroaders, fascinating in its miniature detail, right down to the tiny Skunk logo.

If you lived along the Skunk Train line you could build a station by the track and the train or railcar would stop there.

Waving is obligatory. Railfans wave at everybody: pedestrians, people in cars, fishermen down in the river, kids at camp, anybody. Go on—wave to everyone!

All rails and rolling stock arrived by ship and unloaded onto the wharf at Soldier's Harbor before the railroad reached Willits in 1911.

How do you steer a Skunk railcar? You don't. The track guides the car to its destination, and the motorman controls the engine speed and the brakes.

It's estimated that over time it cost $1,700,000 to build the railroad from Fort Bragg to Willits—nearly $40,000 a mile.

When "Navigation" was part of the California Western Railroad's title there were eight ships working with the trains to deliver finished lumber to market. The *National City*, built in 1888 and purchased in 1906, was sold to Peru in 1918. The *Brunswick* came from Oregon in 1903 and was sold in 1931. The *Coquille River* was Oregon-built in 1896, came south in 1908, and was sold off in 1925. The *Arctic*, which also had come from Oregon in 1908, wrecked off Point Arena in 1922.

Three ships bore the name *Noyo*. Built in Humboldt Bay in 1888, *Noyo #1* wrecked off Point Arena in 1914. *Noyo #2*, built in San Francisco in 1913 smashed up off Point Arena in 1935. Built in Seattle in 1920, *Noyo #3* arrived in 1935 and did not sink off Point Arena. It was sold to Thailand in 1940. All these vessels were steam schooners and built of wood, except for the last two *Noyos*, which were steel-hulled.

Fairmont W110 Dual Tamper adjusts ballast and ties near Irmulco in 1967.
(Noyo Chief *Photo*)

The railroad started with sixty-five-pound rail. Now rail is 90- or 112-pound stock. There are 341 curves in forty miles of track, and some of these curves are thirty degrees. There is a single straight stretch of track one mile long on the line near Shake City. There is a "no man's land" with no road access

*In 1934 Shake City was the last logging camp on the California Western mainline. (*Noyo Chief *Photo)*

from MP 10.3 to MP 18 at Alpine. Climbing a 2.6 percent grade from Shake City through the Horseshoe Curve and the Crowley Loop, the line goes over the mountains at Summit with three percent grades down to Willits.

When the California Western line opened there were 115 bridges. The last of the A-frame bridges, which provided overhead support to prevent damage by logs floating downriver during floods, was replaced in 1963 as the railroad made improvements.

WHISTLE SIGNALS

Each —— is a long toot, each • is a short toot.

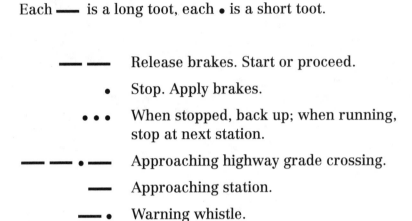

—— ——   Release brakes. Start or proceed.

•   Stop. Apply brakes.

• • •   When stopped, back up; when running, stop at next station.

—— —— • ——   Approaching highway grade crossing.

——   Approaching station.

—— •   Warning whistle.

A number of short toots closely spaced is an alarm for livestock or persons on the track.

ASSORTED WRECKS AND ABANDONED LINES

In January 1936, Engine 23 went as a helper engine on a double-header. Leaving Fort Bragg ahead of the regular train, it crashed through the rails a half mile east of Bridge 10, where heavy rains had washed out the fill beneath the track. Momentum kept the engine going and it plowed into the bank on the other side of the slip-out. The engineer, William King, was thrown clear. The locomotive's cab buckled, pinning fireman Herman Gustafson between the cab and the boiler. Rivets popped out of the boiler due to the collision, and the escaping steam scalded Gustafson to death. In over one hundred years of operation, this was the only fatality to a California Western Railroad crew member ever to occur.

In May 1936, during the Great Depression, an unknown transient met a terrible fate near Shake City. A member of a hobo camp in Fort Bragg, he had started walking eastward along the tracks toward Willits. The morning train from Willits came along and cut him in two when he failed to get off the tracks in time.

In September 1964 two Skunk railcars collided head-on fourteen miles east of Willits near McMullen Creek. Seventy-three passengers and four crewmen were involved, and seventeen people were taken to hospitals. Westbound were thirty-two San Mateo Masonic Lodge members, and eastbound were forty-one members of the Aircraft Pilot's Club of Oakland. The crash tossed passengers about in both cars. Westbound M-80 had overrun its meeting place where it was supposed to have waited for M-100 to pass. The California Western took actions to be sure no similar incident ever occurred again.

Three linked runaway diesel engines derailed in January 1970 after rolling down the grade east of Summit Station. The engineer and fireman tried to stop the lead engine but the air brake failed and they jumped to safety before the engines rolled over into an embankment on a curve. Northwestern Pacific Railroad helped re-rail the engines.

In 1970, at Milepost 15.3 near Camp Three Station, a log slide shoved 300 feet of California Western track downhill toward the Noyo River. The engineer stopped the train before it was

1970 wreck of Engines 51, 52, and 54 after air brakes failed on the grade down to Willits. (Skunk Train Archive)

too late. That left one hundred loaded boxcars of freight stacked up in the rail yard in Fort Bragg after a week during which more than six inches of rain fell.

ABANDONED LINES

GLEN BLAIR REDWOOD COMPANY

This logging concern six miles inland from Fort Bragg started out in 1886 as the Pudding Creek Lumber Company. The mill and town were called Glen Blair. The Union Lumber Company's predecessor, the Fort Bragg Redwood Company, built the Fort Bragg Railroad to that mill in 1887. That railroad became the California Western in 1905.

Union Lumber Company bought this operation in 1903 and renamed it the Glen Blair Redwood Company. A Shay locomotive built by Lima in 1889 was the first engine, with a second Shay purchased in 1907. In 1910 an 0-4-0T engine called the "Dinky" was added. All the lumber this mill produced was shipped by rail to Fort Bragg. In 1913, passenger service let riders leave Fort Bragg at 6 a.m. and arrive in Glen Blair ready to go to work at the break of day.

The Glen Blair operation prospered until the late 1920s when lumber sales fell. The mill closed and the equipment sat until Shay No. 2 was used on the Ten Mile logging railroad in 1941. The tracks were torn up in 1942 from the Glen Blair junction on the California Western to Glen Blair. The Dinky became an exhibition museum piece and is on display in the commercial establishment next to the Fort Bragg depot. Both Shays were scrapped before 1951.

TEN MILE BRANCH

Starting in 1916, Union Lumber Company built a logging railroad along the coast from Fort Bragg, over a high trestle at Pudding Creek, north to the Ten Mile River, then east into miles of timber. Spreading up two forks of the river, rails ended 17.6 miles from Fort Bragg at Camp Six on the Middle Fork and 16.5 miles out at the Clark Fork Landing on the North Fork.

Over the decades, hundreds of people worked in the woods and lived in the camps, but managers everywhere found that trucks could do a better job and go more places than trains. By June 1949 the decision was made to abandon the line. A last excursion train pulled by Engine 14 took loggers and their families out for sightseeing and a lunch at the Camp Two cookhouse.

On June 17, 1949, a three-day extravaganza of rail deconstruction took place as twenty-two miles of railroad on the Ten Mile Branch vanished: 16,869 pieces of angle iron were broken loose from the rails with sledgehammers and chisels; 8,448 rails were pulled up, and 96,000 ties were removed. Woods work was suspended while men worked to remove the rails. In three days a high-speed truck road was created on the railroad roadbed.

CALIFORNIA WESTERN MOTIVE POWER ROSTER

Fort Bragg Railroad, predecessor to the California Western, owned four locomotives numbered 1 to 4. They carried the same numbers when they became California Western engines. Letter "T" indicates a tank engine.

NUMBER 1. Acquired in 1905, Type 2-4-2T, built 1885 by Baldwin. Fort Bragg Railroad named the wood burner the *Sequoia*. She carried that name to the California Western. Sold in 1906 to Standish & Hickey Lumber.

NUMBER 2. Acquired in ?, Type 2-4-2T, built in 1887 by Baldwin. Irvine & Muir Lumber bought this engine in 1910. When a trailing truck from Engine No. 3 was switched, this engine became a 2-4-2T. There were two engines numbered No. 2.

NUMBER 2. Acquired in ?, Type 0-4-2, built in 1901 by Baldwin. Scrapped in 1920, this engine had come from the California State Belt Railroad.

NUMBER 3. Acquired in 1905, Type 2-4-4T, built in 1884 by Baldwin. Mendocino Lumber bought this engine in 1918.

A crane has lifted this engine from a ship and is setting it on rails on the wharf. A wood burner, the engine had been converted to an oil burner in the Bay Area. (Courtesy of Robert Lee, photo historian)

NUMBER 4. Acquired in 1905, Type 4-4-0, Built in 1883 by Hinkley. Southern Pacific supplied this engine, which was scrapped in 1914.

NUMBER 5. Acquired in 1906, Type 4-6-0, built in 1880 by Schenectady. This engine pulled the first passenger train from Fort Bragg to Willits over the newly completed line. Purchased from Southern Pacific of Arizona, it was scrapped in 1923.

NUMBER 6. Acquired in 1908, Type 0-4-0, built in 1868 by Mason. Conflicting origin information. Could have been Santa Fe, Southern Pacific, or California Pacific. Sold in 1910 and scrapped in 1915.

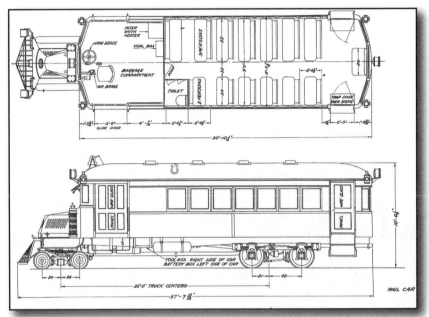

Schematic line drawing of the Skunk Motorcar M-80. (Skunk Train Archive)

NUMBER 7. Acquired in 1909, Type 2-6-2T, built in 1909 by Baldwin. In 1924 this engine was renumbered No. 17.

NUMBER 8. Acquired in 1910, Type 4-6-0, built by Southern Pacific in 1869. Previously used by the Central and Southern Pacific, it was renumbered No. 38 in 1924.

NUMBER 9. Acquired in 1912, Type 3-T Shay, built by Lima Locomotive Works in 1912. White River Lumber bought this engine in 1914 and scrapped it in 1924.

(No Number 10)

NUMBER 11. Acquired in 1913, Type 2-6-2, built in 1913 by Baldwin. It was scrapped in 1947.

NUMBER 12. Acquired in 1914, Type 2-6-2, built in 1914 by Baldwin. It was scrapped in 1950.

(No Number 13)

NUMBER 14. Acquired in 1938, Type 2-6-2T, a tank engine built

in 1924 by Baldwin. Built for the California Fruit Exchange in Graeagle, California, it was purchased by Burt Rudolph of Willits in 1956 and now belongs to the Roots of Motive Power group at the Mendocino County Museum in Willits.

Engine 21 and crew more than fifty years ago. (Kelley House Photo Archive)

(No Numbers 15 or 16)

NUMBER 17. Renumbered No. 7; scrapped in 1938.

(No numbers 18, 19, or 20)

NUMBER 21. Acquired in 1920, Type 2-6-2, built in 1920 by Baldwin. Once used on the Ten Mile Branch in 1950, it was purchased by Pan-American Engineering.

NUMBER 22. Acquired in 1921, Type 2-6-2, built in 1921 by Baldwin. It was scrapped in 1952.

NUMBER 23. Acquired in 1923, Type 2-6-2, built in 1923 by Baldwin. It was scrapped in 1950.

California Western Engine 36, acquired from Colorado Midland Railroad in 1918. (Skunk Train Archive)

(No numbers 23 to 35)

NUMBER 36. Acquired in 1918, Type 4-6-0, built in 1890(?) by Baldwin. Sold to Little River Lumber in 1929, it had been purchased from Colorado Midland Railroad.

(No Number 37)

NUMBER 38 was renumbered No. 8, changed in 1924, and scrapped in 1942.

(No Numbers 39 or 40)

NUMBER 41. Acquired in 1922, Type 0-6-0, built in 1901 by Baldwin. After service on the Arizona & New Mexico Railway and El Paso & Southwestern Railway it came to Fort Bragg and was scrapped in 1937.

NUMBER 41. Acquired in 1940, Type 2-8-0, built in 1920 by Baldwin. Here we go again: like Engine No. 2, there were two locomotives with the same number. From the Sierra Railroad, it was scrapped in 1950.

(No Numbers 42 or 43)

NUMBER 44. Acquired in 1944, Type 2-8-2, built in 1930 by Baldwin. Coming from Lamm Lumber at Modoc Point, Oregon, it was scrapped in 1952.

NUMBER 45. Acquired in 1964, Type 2-8-2, built in 1924 by Baldwin. The Super Skunk! Medford Corporation in Oregon supplied the Mikado-style engine rebuilt in 1964 for the California Western.

*Three Baldwin diesel locomotives before a freight run in 1958. (*Noyo Chief *Photo)*

NUMBER 46. Acquired in 1968, Type 2-6-6-2, built in 1937 by Baldwin. A Mallet engine built for Weyerhauser Timber and used by Rayonier.

(No numbers 47–50)

NUMBERS 51 AND 52. Acquired in 1949, diesels, built in 1949 by Baldwin. DS-4-4-, 1000 horsepower. Both were scrapped after a 1970 accident involving No. 54.

NUMBER 53. Acquired in 1969, diesel, built in 1949 by Baldwin. Acquired from Pan-American Engineering. Sold to John Bradley in Willits, it is now part of Roots of Motive Power's collection.

NUMBER 54. Acquired in 1969, diesel, built in 1949 by Baldwin. Scrapped with Numbers 51 and 52 after a 1970 accident. Built for the Wabash Railroad.

Passenger Coach interior awaiting railfans. (Skunk Train Archive)

NUMBERS 55 AND 56. Acquired in 1970, diesels, built in 1955 by Baldwin for the McCloud River Railroad; No. 55 was replaced in 1987; No. 56 was sold in 1985 to John Bradley in Willits for parts to rebuild engine No. 53.

NUMBER 57. Acquired in 1970, diesel, built in 1955 by Baldwin for Southern Pacific.

(No Numbers 58 to 60)

NUMBERS 61, 62 AND 63. Acquired in 1976, diesels, built in 1955 by Alco. All Alco RS11 Road Switchers built for Southern Pacific. Replaced in 1987.

NUMBERS 64, 65, AND 66. Acquired in the 1990s. All were EMD GP-9 diesels, built for Southern Pacific in the 1950s. Number 66 came from Golden Spike Industries in New York.

MOTORCARS

M-80. Acquired in 1925, built in 1923 by Mack. Mack Trucks built this as a demonstration vehicle in 1923 and carried forty-five passengers. It was scrapped in 1964 after a collision with M-100. The designation "M" meant it carried its own motive power, and the number refers to the rated horsepower at the time of purchase.

M-100. Acquired in 1934, built in 1925 by Edwards Motor Cars. Morehead & North Fork Railroad in Kentucky provided this thirty-six-passenger rail bus in 1934. Its two 60-horsepower Buda four-cylinder gas engines were replaced in 1946 with a 150-horsepower Cummins diesel. It was rebuilt in 1956 by the California Western to provide increased visibility and comfort.

M-100 Motorcar crossing the Noyo. (Skunk Train Archive)

M-200. Acquired in 1941, built in 1927 by the Skagit Iron & Steel Company in Washington State for the Longview, Portland & Northern Railway in 1927. It was purchased from the Trona Railway in 1941. Its dual six-cylinder, 150-horsepower Buda engine was replaced with a Cummins 156-horsepower diesel in 1955. In 1975 it was donated to the Pacific Locomotive Society Museum, then at Castro Point, after being retired from Skunk Train service. This museum is now the Niles Canyon Railway, and M-200 runs there.

M-300. Acquired in 1963, built in 1935 by American Car. After service on North Carolina's Aberdeen & Rockfish Railroad and on the Saltair Route in Utah, it arrived on the Skunk line in 1963. A 220-horsepower Cummins diesel replaced the original six-cylinder, 168-horsepower Hall-Scott gas engine.

COACHES

Finding coaches for the early Redwood Route was a problem. Track curves disallowed using long coaches. Four coaches, seventy-two feet long and seating eighty passengers, were obtained from the Erie & Lackawanna Railroad in Pennsylvania. Built in 1926 by the Standard Steel Car Company, they were named the Cleone, Navarro, Sherwood, and Noyo after rebuilding. Two coaches added years later bore the names Westport and DeHaven.

The Skunk no longer names its coaches. Today's nine coaches were built to be commuter cars for the Southern Pacific Railroad and were acquired in the 1990s. The observation cars are old coaches with their tops removed.

ROLLING STOCK

It takes a lot of maintenance equipment to keep Skunk trains rolling. Behind the scenes in the shops and train yard you'd find a gigantic 1955 burro crane, a tie inserter/extractor, track liner, track tamper, ballast regulator, flatcars, bulkhead flatcar, belly-dump gravel car, a caboose, and an old pile driver at Northspur.

Available for excursions are three diesel engines, one steam locomotive, six coaches, two open observation cars, and one concession car.

In 1912, when servicing the mills, California Western had hundreds of cars including 156 flatcars, three boxcars, six tank cars, and a stock car. In the 1930s the line had fifty-four freight cars.

SIDINGS AND SPURS

There are sidings where trains can pass each other at Ranch, Alpine, Burbeck, and Crowley, along with yards in Fort Bragg and Willits. There are, or have been, dead-end spurs at Glen Blair, South Fork, Rockpit, Grove, Camp Three, Alpine, Northspur (with a "Y"), Irmulco, Shake City, Burbeck, Clare Mill, Summit, and Sage Spur.

Motorcar M-200 rolling down the rails. (Skunk Train Archive)

BIBLIOGRAPHY

Borden, Stanley. "California Western Railroad." *Western Railroader*, XX–8, 1957.

_____."Glen Blair Redwood Company and Cleone Tramway." *Western Railroader*, XXVI–9, 1961.

Brooks, Jerry. *Blowing Smoke Up The Noyo*. Ripon: Beyond Words, undated.

Carranco, Lynwood and Labbe, John T. *Logging the Redwoods*. Caldwell: Caxton Publishing, 1979.

_____. *Redwood Lumber Industry*. San Marino: Golden West, 1982.

Crump, Spencer. *Redwoods, Iron Horses and the Pacific*. Glendale: Trans-Anglo, 1965.

_____. *Skunk Railroad*. Glendale: Trans-Anglo, 1983.

Levene, Bruce and Miklose, Sally. *Fort Bragg Remembered*. Mendocino: Pacific Transcriptions, 1989.

McNairn, Jack and MacMuller, Jerry. *Ships of the Redwood Coast*. Stanford: Stanford University Press, 1949.

Mendocino County Historical Society. *Mills of Mendocino County*. Ukiah: Mendocino County Historical Society, 1996.

Mendocino Historical Review. *1906 Quake*. Mendocino: Mendocino Historical Research, 1980.

Noyes, Charles G. *Redwood Lumbering in California Forests*. San Francisco: Edgar Cherry and Company, 1884.

Palmer, Lyman. *History of Mendocino County California*. San Francisco: Alley, Bowen and Company, 1880.

Ryder, David. *Memories of the Mendocino Coast*. San Francisco: Taylor and Taylor, 1966.

Westing, Fred. *Locomotives That Baldwin Built*. Seattle: Superior Publishing, 1966.

Winn, Robert. *Mendocino Indian Reservation*. Mendocino: Mendocino Historical Research. 1986.

Wurm, Ted. *Mallets on the Mendocino Coast*. Glendale: Trans-Anglo, 1986.

ACKNOWLEDGEMENTS

Thanks to Robert J. Pinoli of Sierra Railroad Company for recognizing the need for such a book, and to Chuck Whitlock, conductor, for Skunk lore.

Thanks to Robert Lee, Mendocino County's extraordinary photo historian, for encouragement, and to the California State Library for a policy of sharing photos.

Photos also came from the Kelley House Museum in Mendocino and the *Noyo Chief* publication of Union Lumber Company/Boise Cascade/Georgia-Pacific.

Thanks to Elizabeth Petersen of Mendocino Graphics for taking words and images and crafting them into a package, and to Joe Shaw of Cypress House for his fine editorial skills.

And Thanks to my husband of 32 years, David Tahja, who encouraged me to write the book and proofread it for train fact accuracy.

Author Katy Tahja dressed in historical costume aboard Engine 45, the Super Skunk.

ABOUT THE AUTHOR

A librarian, author and historian, Katy Tahja has traveled 20,000 miles on AMTRAK and VIA RAIL. This is the first of several trackside guides she plans to write. Tahja's next book, *Early Mendocino Coast*, will be published by Arcadia Publishing in September 2008. It features many photos of local railroading. Home is the village of Comptche in Mendocino County, where her family has lived for 120 years.

Willits Depot

Fort Bragg Depot

HOW TO REACH THE DEPOTS

WILLITS: From Highway 101 turn east on Commercial Street and drive three blocks. The depot is on your right at 299 East Commercial. Phone is 707-459-5248. Look both ways before you cross the tracks!

FORT BRAGG: From Highway 1 turn west on Laurel Street. Drive one block. Phone is 707-964-6371.

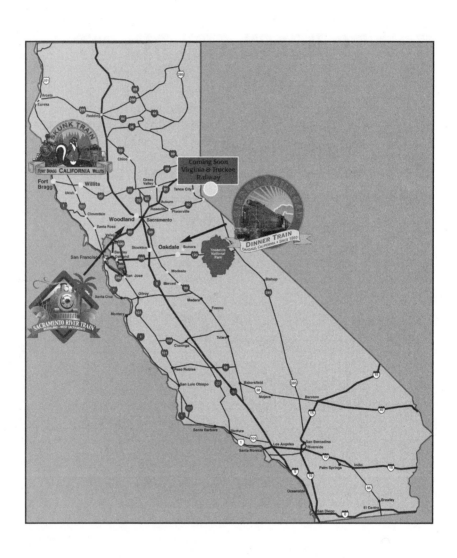

SISTER RAILROADS

The **Sierra Railroad Company** serves as the parent company for all operations and was built in 1897, connecting the Gold Country and Central Valley. As one of the oldest railroads in North America, the Sierra continues to haul freight, carry passengers, make Hollywood movies, and play an important role in California history.

From the redwoods of the north coast to the mighty Sacramento River and the Stanislaus River valley, we invite you to see California while experiencing rail travel at its finest.

Regarded as one of the five best dinner trains in the West, the **Sierra Railroad Dinner Train**, launched in 1999, provides visitors an opportunity to travel on the historic Sierra Railroad while enjoying a delicious meal, beautiful countryside, and a wide range of entertainment. Every week of the year, the Dinner Train offers romantic dinners, fun murder mysteries, lunches, Sunday brunches, wild west shows, wine tasting, and much more. Our train station in Oakdale is conveniently located one-plus hour from the San Francisco Bay Area or Sacramento, on the way toward Yosemite National Park. Open year-round with two hundred-plus trips, Sierra Railroad offers a rich variety of excursions for adults, families or groups. www.SierraRailroad.com

The **Sacramento RiverTrain** offers food and entertainment while you roll through the countryside. This new train features a sparkling gold exterior—reflecting the area's Gold Rush heritage—and 1,000 feet of blue waves that are a tribute to the Sacramento River which the train's route follows. Popular sights include the Sacramento River and the 8,000-foot-long Fremont Trestle. The train is ideal for both daytime and evening trips because it features open-air observation cars, an open-air patio bar, a high-level dining coach, and fun club car. While you roll along, enjoy a great combination of scenery, food, and entertainment. The Club Car features live music on our weekend RiverTrain Dinner Parties. Twice a month we offer a fun "Murder Mystery Dinner." The open-air cars are popular during Saturday "Great Train Robberies" or Sunday Champagne brunches. Located fifteen minutes from Sacramento, the train boards in Woodland, California. Trips are offered every week of the year. www.SacramentoRiverTrain.com

In 2006 Sierra was unanimously selected by the Nevada Commission for the Reconstruction of the Virginia & Truckee Railway to become the operators of this world class line. Scheduled to open around 2011, the **Virginia & Truckee Railway** will be an exciting ride through the historic mining areas of Nevada while the Sierra Nevada Mountains serve as a mighty backdrop.

For more information, seasonal trips, special events and updated schedules, please visit our three linked websites or call us until 8:00 p.m. any day of the week, 800-866-1690. www.SierraRailroad.com